Presented to

Colby

by

Tony

on

Ronnie

© 1993 Christine Harder Tangvald.
© 2003 Standard Publishing, Cincinnati, Ohio.
A division of Standex International Corporation.
All rights reserved.
Sprout logo is a trademark of Standard Publishing.
Printed in Italy.
Design: Marypat Pino.
Scripture verses adapted from the *Good News Bible
in Today's English Version– Second Edition,*
Copyright © 1992 by American Bible Society.
Used by Permission.
ISBN 0-7847-1285-9

09 08 07
9 8 7 6 5 4 3

The BEST Thing About Easter

written by Christine Harder Tangvald
illustrated by C.A. Nobens

Standard
PUBLISHING
CINCINNATI, OHIO

Do you like Easter? **I DO!** I think Easter is **FUN!**
I like to dye Easter eggs all different colors—
pink ones, and green ones, and blue ones, and
orange ones, and yellow ones.

Which one is **YOUR** favorite?

Then, after we dye the eggs …

...we **HIDE** them!

I love to hunt for Easter eggs, don't you?

Here's one, right here! How many can you find? Yes, I think Easter eggs are fun!

But Easter eggs aren't the **BEST thing about Easter!**

Sometimes we have **CANDY** Easter eggs with soft, squishy marshmallow on the inside. Sometimes we have gooey, chewy jelly beans that taste like lemon or cherry or peppermint! Yum, yum, yum!

And sometimes we have dark chocolate Easter bunnies that melt in your mouth!

I like Easter candy . . . **A LOT!**

But candy isn't the **BEST thing about Easter.**

Did you ever pet a soft, furry bunny at Easter time?
I did—at my uncle's farm. I like soft, furry bunnies.

Once my cousin got a fuzzy yellow duck that said, "Quack, quack, quack!"

My other cousin got a cute baby chick that said, "Peep, peep, peep!"

I like furry bunnies and fuzzy ducks and cute baby chicks, don't you?

But bunnies and ducks and chicks aren't the **BEST thing about Easter.**

Easter is in the springtime, and guess what happens **THEN!**
I run, run, run on the green, green grass, **UP** the hill and **DOWN**
the hill in the bright, warm sunshine.

Whee!! Just **WATCH** me! Everything is bursting with new life in the springtime.

But springtime isn't the **BEST thing about Easter.**

I like to get **ALL DRESSED UP** on Easter Sunday, don't you?
First I scrub, scrub, scrub in the tub and get all clean.

Then I brush, brush, brush my hair. And then I put on my **VERY BEST CLOTHES!**

Wow! Just look at me! I look terrific!

Then at church on Easter Sunday, we talk and laugh together.
We sit and sing together, and we listen and pray together.
We have a great time together too.

Oh, **YES!** I like getting all dressed up and being together on Easter Sunday.

But even that isn't the **BEST** thing about Easter.

The very **BEST THING** about Easter is . . .

JESUS!
God's own Son!

Oh, yes! Jesus is the **BEST THING** about Easter.

You see, we have Easter because of Jesus.
Easter is about something wonderful that was
part of God's **AMAZING** plan.

First, a very sad thing happened.
Jesus died on the cross.

But guess what! Jesus did not stay dead!
No, he **DID NOT!**

On the very first Easter morning, God made Jesus **ALIVE** again! The tomb was **EMPTY!**

Jesus' friends were **SO** surprised and **SO** happy to see him again.

"Jesus is alive!" they said. "He is really alive!"

And then, a little later, do you know what God did?

He took Jesus up, up, up ... right through a cloud into **HEAVEN!**
It was all part of **GOD'S** amazing plan!

But the **MOST** amazing part of God's plan
is that Jesus died and lives again…for **ME!**

It's **TRUE!** Because Jesus loves me, you see.
He loves **YOU** too.

> "This is what love is:
> God loved us and
> sent His Son."
>
> 1 John 4:10

Oh yes! I like Easter eggs, and I like Easter candy, and I like soft furry bunnies and fuzzy baby ducks, and I like getting all dressed up and being together on Easter Sunday.

BUT . . .

...the **BEST THING** about Easter is Jesus!

I'm **GLAD** Jesus loves me!

I'm really, **REALLY** glad, aren't you?

Happy Easter, everyone!